STEPPING UP IN LEADERSHIP

Reflections from the journey

STEPPING UP IN LEADERSHIP

Reflections from the journey

Jo Koepke

Editing by Emma-Lee Hazeldean, with input from Lexia Smallwood and Tiffany Edmonds

Cover photo by Alex Rodríguez Santibáñez on Unsplash

ISBN: 978-0-646-80351-7
eISBN: 978-0-646-80352-4

All enquiries about this publication and speaking engagements: enquiries@jokoepke.com
Website: jokoepke.com
Facebook: @jokoepke
Instagram: @jokoepke

DEDICATION

For my incredible daughter, Isabel.
Being your mother is my highest leadership calling.
May you always fight through your fear,
love with passion,
and lead with compassion and courage.
Remember that you are strong.
You are courageous.
You can do hard things.

Contents

Why this book?

My mobile phone rings. I know there is little battery left and I run to my bedroom to plug it in. I answer the phone leaning on the edge of my bed, with the power cord stretched as far as it goes. The voice at the other end is one I know well. The question she asks me is to take on the next stage in the rocket blast of leadership. I feel my legs tremble and I sit straight on the floor. Has she called the right person? Surely she meant to call someone else! I look around at the overflowing laundry hamper, the toys I can see in the lounge and the bag that serves as my filing system. I take my next brave step and agree to pray about it and discuss it with my husband.

Being asked to consider the State Leader role came out of the blue and was a catalyst to further evaluate what I knew about leadership and what it would take for me to be effective if I said yes.

If you had told me the year before that I would be transitioning into the MOPS[1] Western Australia State Leader[2] position, I would have told you that you had the wrong person. I had no concept of the journey I would find myself on over that year and where I would continue to find myself in subsequent years. At the time, I was on the leadership team at my local MOPS group. I was also helping to organise the State Conference as my friend had taken on the Conference Coordinator role. Shortly after the conference in October 2015, I was approached to take on the Region Leader[3] role for the northern suburbs of my city. This mainly involved being a support to the Coordinators and other leaders of the groups, training them and helping to resolve issues.

I wrestled with the decision. I had to fight feeling inadequate, debate if my schedule could accommodate the extra responsibilities and assess whether my family would cope with the extra weekends away from them. I discussed it with my husband, parents and trusted friends. I prayed and listened. Then I summoned my courage and said yes to the Region Leader position. I had only been a Region Leader for a term when I received that next call to ask me to consider taking over the State Leader role for the following year.

Little did I know that the journey would not end there. A few months into my State Leader role, we were working through training on succession planning. The MOPS Field Manager at the time asked me and a couple of others to keep her role in mind as a possibility for future years when she was ready to step down. None of us had an inkling that the moment would come within six months. Making this decision generated another season of wrestling, praying and discussing. Once more, the answer was yes.

I have already learned so much in the process of considering and

[1] Mothers of Preschoolers-- find out more at mops.org.au

[2] Oversees all MOPS groups in a state, recruits, trains and supports Region Leaders, provides administrative oversight and conflict resolution support, and plans the leadership training for the annual State Conference.

[3] Supports and trains the Coordinators and leaders of 3-6 MOPS groups in a region

transitioning into each new role. The more I discover, the more I have questions and ponderings to be answered. I make no claim to be an expert in leadership. I can only share the experience and knowledge I have gained in my journey so far. This journey has ignited a passion for leadership within me and a passion to bring other women like me along for the ride.

This book was originally birthed through the Write 31 Days Challenge 2016, where the aim was to write every day in October. This was my third year writing for the challenge. I was undecided about participating, after an intense few months leading up to October. Three weeks before the challenge, I attended the Fresh Leadership Conference here in Perth. I had been sick and barely made it to the conference but felt strongly that I needed to be there. Within the first hour, I had a download experience—the concept and basic outline for a series on leadership filled my mind. When God spoke in that way, I had to choose to be obedient.

I want to take you on this journey with me to explore what I have learned about leadership, the challenges I've faced, the resources I turn to and what I still want to learn. Maybe you have been in leadership for a long time and want to see through fresh eyes. Maybe you are like me and are taking steps to a new level of leadership. Maybe you don't even see yourself as a leader but something inside of you is drawn to this concept. My heart is to inspire and encourage you, while I reflect and learn myself.

What is leadership?

A book on leadership can hardly begin without a discussion on what leadership means. Far greater minds than mine have wrestled with the many questions surrounding who is a leader. In the reading and listening I have done, I recognise the core elements that seem to come through from several sources and ring true to my own experience.

Influence

A leader may have a title but if they have no influence over those they are meant to lead, it is a title only. Conversely, there are many leaders wielding great influence (for good and bad) who do not have a title or position. John C. Maxwell's definition of a leader puts this simply: *"Leadership is influence"*.

Who is it in your life that you have influence over? When I reflect on this in my own life, the most obvious answer is my daughter. Being a parent is synonymous with being a leader in my mind. It is, by far, the greatest leadership calling I have. I need to remember that when the demands and responsibilities of other positions crowd in.

It is also easy to come up with answers to this question within the defined positions I hold. It is clearly marked out who I have been assigned influence over—the colleagues I oversee in my paid work and the leaders in my MOPS roles. I feel the weight of this, especially in my MOPS role. To be commissioned into a position of influence at a national level humbles me and daunts me. The challenge is to use that influence effectively and not rely on a title.

I sometimes stop and wonder about those I have influence over without even realising it. For example, our online world allows access to others we will never meet. My words have the ability to influence people around the world while I sleep or go about my day. Closer to home, I meet with friends, acquaintances and even strangers. What influence do I have there? What influence do you have there?

If your actions inspire others to dream more, learn more, do more and become more, you are a leader. —*John Quincy Adams*

Servant

Many in positions of leadership assume their title gives them the right to be waited on and to lord it over those in their influence—that somehow the title imbues them with greater worth than others. My own view of leadership goes against this, however, I may have to battle my pride on this matter at times!

The first responsibility of a leader is to define reality. The last is to say thank you. In between, the leader is a servant. —Max DePree

To command is to serve, nothing more and nothing less. —*Andre Malraux*

No matter how prestigious or non-existent the title, a leader is a servant of those they lead. It pays not to forget that.

For me, I look to the Bible and Jesus' example of this to inform the kind of leader I strive to be. Throughout Scripture, Jesus demonstrates this servant leadership. He laid everything down for those he was leading. He expected no special treatment. He went against social norms to reach out to those who were shunned and to demonstrate how to lead others —like washing his disciples' feet (John 13). All of this was born out of love, even for those who would betray Him. As a Christian in leadership, I want that love to be the defining factor in my leadership journey too. I especially want this to be true with those that I may not naturally get along with.

Vision and direction

> *Where there is no vision, the people perish. —Proverbs 29:18 KJV*

It is a leader's responsibility to set the vision for those they influence. It is not enough to hold the vision; it needs to be communicated in such a way that people can catch it and run with it.

> *Leadership is the capacity to translate vision into reality. —Warren Bennis*

> *You don't lead by pointing and telling people some place to go. You lead by going to that place and making a case. —Ken Kesey*

Before a vision can be communicated, it has to be well developed and certain in your own mind. It requires creativity, wisdom, and the ability to see beyond the here and now. In my position, it also requires a close relationship with God to hear from Him.

Made and developed

The idea that a leader is born can be a tough, ingrained belief to shift. Leaders are not born but are made and developed. It is easy to look at people who seem to be able to gather people naturally, have 'bossy' tendencies or are extroverts, and label them 'born leaders'. There may well be natural inclinations there but they will come to nought if not developed. I have often discounted my own ability to be a leader due to my introverted nature. More on that to come.

Empowering others

A true leader seeks to raise up other leaders rather than see them as a threat. Their eyes are always seeking the one who could take their place and on the lookout for potential leaders. This is close to my heart in the MOPS position I hold.

For me, these are the core elements of leadership. So many other aspects can be drawn in to fill out the picture but these are my essentials. Maybe in your own life you have recognised areas of leadership from this list that you hadn't recognised previously. Perhaps it has highlighted areas to be worked on like this exercise has for me. Your list of essentials may differ from mine. I encourage you to take the time to define leadership for yourself. This will form the basis of your own leadership journey.

Your Turn

Use this space to define leadership for yourself and reflect on those in your life over whom you have influence.

One key thought I want to remember:

What drives you to lead where you are?

A great leader's courage to fulfill his vision comes from passion, not position.
—John C. Maxwell

I love this quote from John C. Maxwell. I have seen this truth repeated in my own life and in the lives of those around me. I have been in positions where I have lost the passion I had when I first began, and have just gone through the motions. I may still fulfil the basic requirements, but the drive to excel is missing and those around me and under my influence suffer for it.

In any role, it can be easy to be worn out by the mundane parts—by life in general—and forget why you're investing your time and energy. I am aware of this challenge to sustain the passion and momentum in my own journey. One factor that I feel helps this in MOPS is that every person involved here in Australia is a volunteer. There has to be a passion for this ministry that drives each leader as there is no monetary gain to be had. (Of course, working as and with volunteers brings other challenges and there is a shadow side to our motivations. More on that later.) We each bring a story of why we invest our time and energy into the area we lead in. This is mine.

Why MOPS? The simple answer for me is that I have experienced the impact of this ministry for myself. My journey with MOPS began shortly after the birth of my daughter who is now seven years old. Those early days are a blur thanks to the intense sleep deprivation impacting my memory development. Motherhood was a far greater challenge than I had anticipated. My daughter had severe reflux, colic and multiple food intolerances that were not picked up well by medical professionals. It took a long time to get any semblance of management happening. Her food intolerances required me to be on a very strict diet while breastfeeding. We later discovered she also had a tongue and lip tie that had gone undiagnosed despite multiple visits to medical professionals. Sleep issues were (and sometimes still are) a significant part of our days despite all the best advice. When your child is in constant pain and going through six sheet changes and up to twenty outfits a day, a sleep routine is a difficult goal to achieve. Added to these issues as she grew were anxiety issues and sensory processing issues. While I know that many face far more significant problems with their kids, it does not lessen the impact these issues caused for our family.

Dealing with these issues, particularly the sleep deprivation, had me in a dark place. I was never formally diagnosed with depression. I am ashamed to say I lied on assessments I was given to stay under the radar —I could not face it. Do not do what I did! I used to wonder how anyone could shake a baby. I now have insight into how that could happen. I know first-hand that it can be the difference between a split second reaction or the decision to walk away and take a break. I have experienced scary thoughts of needing to put my daughter up for adoption because I wasn't capable, which quickly turned into *no one else would handle it either so I had better just put both of us out of our misery*. I am so grateful that those thoughts were fleeting. Throughout these challenges, I had the support of my amazing husband and family. And there was MOPS.

At MOPS, I found a community that took me in, gave me a break from my daughter and encouraged me. We were in the trenches together and I could talk with others who understood where I was at. They gave me the boost each fortnight that I needed. Making deep friends has never been easy for this introvert and now I have dear friends who have come from this community. As I was emerging from the worst of the fog, it became more than just an encouragement in my parenting journey. I felt invested in as a woman and as a person; that I was not just a parent. I was reminded that my abilities and giftings were not lost despite the season I was in. I found opportunities to be involved and realised that I did not have to wait until my daughter was older to be involved in leadership. I was not stuck, as I had been feeling.

Why MOPS? I have been invested in by other leaders. I have experienced the all-round growth in my own life. I have experienced community in a way that is often missing in our society these days. I now have the opportunity to support and train leaders to create space for other women to experience that encouragement and community at a national level. What an immense privilege! My heart and the heart of MOPS is for this community to show the love of Jesus in a tangible way, to show what everyday life walking in relationship with God can look like. We want women to feel supported, encouraged, equipped and, most importantly, loved by Jesus. This is the passion that I come back to in my own leadership journey. This is what drives me past the obstacles I encounter and will keep encountering. This is what I hope will allow me to have the courage to fulfil the vision.

Can you see that progression in your life of being served, growing and then serving others? I can look back over my journey and see the people who have invested in me. Their role in my own life inspires me to do the same for others. Look back over your own journey. Where have you felt served? Who can you point to at those times and places? This pattern is the undercurrent of our passion and drive. We get to be a part of that pattern for others.

What story do you bring to your own leadership role, whether you have a title or not? What passion drives you? I encourage you to write it down and come back to it when your passion begins to wane. We all need that reminder. We also need to be on the look-out for new stories that drive us, fresh moments to fuel our passion.

The shadow side of what drives you

That story of what drives you is essential. However, a look at drivers wouldn't be complete without looking at the shadow side. This dark undercurrent runs through our decision making and our reactions. I am finding that progress on this journey as a leader is strongly linked to how aware I am of these underlying motivators, and how I am seeking transformation from my default to my best.

The more I explore this concept of underlying drivers, the more I see *fear* as the basis of many of them. This fear morphs into so many different forms, speaking to each of us in a different way, knowing just which buttons to push. To some, fear may talk about making mistakes, not measuring up or failing. To others, fear may speak of obscurity, missing out or being passed over. Not enough. Too much. Unqualified. Too broken. Unloveable. It can clamour loudly or whisper, be all-consuming or be unrecognised and subtle.

I am convinced of our need to recognise the presence of fear in our motivations. Fear is a liar and can drive us into roles that were not meant for us, or to work in ways that hurt ourselves and those around us. Or maybe fear of the unknown keeps you in a place for far longer than is healthy for you or those you work with. When we see the fear at work, we can bring truth and support to combat those fears. It allows us to make decisions from a place of strength and wholeness.

I find myself in one of these situations again. For the past few years, I have been restless in my job. I have switched roles, negotiated changes to tap into my passion areas more and tried to ignore the nudge to end this season. Over nine years of my working life have been spent with this company. I switched careers to join all those years ago and sense a big shift once more. Fear of the unknown and not having a clear next step in front of me fuelled the desire to ignore and stay put. I have reached the point where I acknolwedge the end of a season. I still do not know what is next but I am actively pursuing change and setting time frames to end this season. I will not let fear of the unknown keep me in a place that is no longer mine.

Conversely, I have also experienced times of almost saying no when I should have said yes because I was waiting until there was no shadow side to my motivations. If there was a trace of pride or fear detected, I thought that meant I had the wrong motivation. I have learned to give myself more grace for being human. The choice to write this book was an example of this. My shadow side whispered that I desire acclaim for my words, that my pride is driving this work. My greater motivation was to encourage and equip other women in their leadership journey. My heart burned with the desire to inspire those who do not see themselves as leaders and those who are stepping up in leadership. I wanted what I have learned to help others. I said yes to publishing these words despite the darker motivations I sensed.

The reality is that none of us is completely free of a shadow side in our decision making. The discernment we need to have is whether that shadow side is the main driver, or a back seat passenger. I have found that this process oftens needs to be in consultation with people who know you well and have the ability to speak truth into your blind spots.

Your Turn

Write down your story of what drives you.

Now explore the shadow side of that drive. Get honest and vulnerable about what is underlying your decision making and reactions.

Can you see the intricate threads of leadership?

Have you ever wondered how you ended up in a particular leadership position? I have those moments of stopping and being completely in awe of where I am. It can feel like it has come out of nowhere. Have you taken the time to reflect back on your life and see the threads of leadership and preparation that have carried you here? In preparing for this book, I have thought about this often. I look back over my life and see these threads suddenly illuminated that I hadn't considered before. I see moments in time that I have dismissed as inconsequential, that now add up to a bigger picture. I hear God's whispered encouragement—that He has been preparing me and drawing out leadership skills long before I considered myself a leader.

My earliest memory of a leadership role is when I was about eleven years old and running praise and worship for the toddler ministry at church on a Sunday. Several other roles in the intervening years have also been in children's and youth ministries. I didn't see these positions as leadership but rather just having a heart for children and youth. The positions were simply a way to be involved. And yet I see skills being developed in administration, getting along with other people, setting goals and vision and being accountable to those I served under. I experienced the influence of many leaders who I learned from —watching both the ways they did things well and the ways I wouldn't want to emulate.

I had inklings that God was calling me to ministry opportunities. I confess that pride became a factor. It was a strange wrestle between the pride of desiring a title and not wanting to accept the label of leader. In my late teens, I made some poor decisions when it came to relationships that derailed my life for a while. Deep down, I was convinced that these choices had permanently disqualified me from any plans that God may have previously had for me. Once life had settled back down again, I returned to serving in church ministries and even held leadership positions with a title. The belief that I had forfeited my purpose in life still lingered underneath it all. This was slowly chipped away at by God's truth and by my seeking help to resolve the deep hurt that was left festering in my soul.

Leadership became a part of my life again and was working its way into my identity when I became a mother. Enter another time of feeling derailed and disqualified in life. I felt completely constrained by the high needs of a little human who depended on me for everything. I felt stuck and sidelined until I began to accept the incredible importance and influence that had been given to me with the title 'mother'. Even when I had worked through the frustration of feeling trapped by motherhood, there was still a pull on my heart for something else.

I share a glimpse into what came next in the "Why this book?" chapter. This gives you a little more insight into the journey. I had been attending MOPS and loved it. The time came that I had to return to work on the day that MOPS ran, so I stepped back for a time. I longed to return. My first 'role' for MOPS was running the audiovisual for the leaders' conference being hosted at my church. I remember sitting at the back listening to the speakers and feeling my heart stir. I longed for more. I had no idea that my leadership journey was about to go full throttle! I was still working and only attended meetings on a rare occasion for the following year. I gave a talk on messy play at one of the sessions because it was something that I love doing. In August or September of that year, 2014, I was approached about coming on the team to help run the MOPS group. I was able to rearrange my work days for 2015 and said yes. I loved being involved and could feel deep growth happening. It was not without its challenges as I came into a new role on the team and instigated changes to the way things had been done before.

That same year, my good friend took on the State Conference Coordinator role. I agreed to join the conference team to help with the decor. As tiring and time-consuming as it was, I felt part of my soul coming alive. Shortly after conference had wrapped up in October 2015, I received a phone call from the State Leader asking me to consider becoming a Region Leader. (The Region Leader role involved becoming a support person and leadership coach for the coordinators of MOPS groups in my region). I was astounded and took some time to pray and talk through this decision. I said yes. When I was again approached by the State Leader barely 6 months later to consider taking on the State Leader role, I sat on the floor in shock. When I was asked to consider the Field Manager postion less than a year after starting the State Leader role, I laughed. A whirlwind of leadership progress. And yet on reflection, I can see how there has been a lifetime of foundations that have been laid to prepare me for this point.

So many factors, people, positions and experiences have formed who I am and the leadership position I now hold. It is impossible to convey to you all of the nuances of these—I do not need to. My heart's desire is for you to take a deeper look at your own life, especially if you struggle to see yourself as a leader. Look through fresh eyes to see the threads of leadership that are being woven together. Speak to your close friends, family and mentors around you about what gifts they see. You might be surprised by what you discover.

The biggest barrier to saying yes: feeling inadequate

By far the biggest struggles I have faced in making the decision to step into a greater leadership role are internal. It is a heart cry I have heard in having conversations with other leaders. We feel inadequate and unqualified. We feel like frauds who may be discovered at any moment. Why would someone possibly want me in this role? I'm not capable of doing this. That feeling rises up even now that I have been working in my current role for a while, and has left me close to a panic attack on several occasions.

We are so quick to look at our own faults and every little reason that might disqualify us. Others often see attributes in us that we are blinded to. I may not have had the courage to say yes if it wasn't for the voices of those people encouraging me and calling out the leadership they saw. Their words of affirmation and confirmation of my calling boosted me. I return to those conversations in my mind whenever the feeling of inadequacy rises within me.

So often we can look at other leaders and think that they have it all together, that they are confident and could not possibly feel inadequate. I am learning more and more how wrong that view is. I love reading and listening to the honest and raw writing and teaching of leaders that I admire. I am recognising more and more how human they are. That sounds strange, but I realised how much I have put leaders on a pedestal and separated them in mind. Maybe that is part of why I struggled to accept the title of leader—I didn't class myself in the same league. I absorbed the tendency of our culture to do that, without being conscious of it. Maybe you have done the same.

The recognition that many leaders feel this sense of inadequacy has developed the idea that there is a benefit to this feeling. If I allow that feeling to paralyse me and stop me moving forward then I miss out on that benefit. That sense of inadequacy can help me to take a healthy look at myself, but only if I work on developing the firm foundation of knowing who I am. I am not perfect. I am not an expert on all things leadership. I have so much to learn. And that is okay. As a Christian leader, I recognise that feeling stretched in a role ensures that I pursue God for the answers and the strength. It deepens my dependence on Him to accomplish the work He has for this ministry. As much as I hate this feeling at times, I have come to accept that I do not ever want to feel completely comfortable in any role. That opens the door to limiting God in His work as I operate out of my own strength.

A caveat I would add is that feeling inadequate is different to a genuine assessment that a role is beyond your capacity in that season. I had to assess whether it was only fear holding me back, or genuine issues with capacity, or not being called to the position. Whenever you are faced with an opportunity, take the time to dig through your initial reactions to what is driving them.

One resource that was brought to my attention while I battled the initial waves of inadequacy was Steven Furtick's book *Unqualified*. The truth I gained from reading that book confirmed so much of what I had felt God impressing on my heart. If you are like me and face this battle, it may help you like it has helped me.

Maybe God wants to do something beyond your abilities, and he is far less intimidated by your failures and limits than you are.
— Steven Furtick

Your Turn

Think through your life. Note down any threads of leadership that you see emerging.

What would you say is your biggest barrier to saying yes to leadership?

Reflect on how much of this is a genuine cause to say no and how much needs to be worked through so you can say yes.

What truth can you cling to?

Weighing up the impact on relationships

Accepting a leadership position means accepting on behalf of your family and close friends too. Every yes requires you to say no to other things. Weighing up the impact on my relationships, especially with my husband and daughter, was a big priority in the decision to step up into a new leadership role. It came close to being a no because of this. The pull of feeling called but hearing the reluctance of my family and changes it would mean to our lives was difficult to navigate. I firmly believe that family needs to be top priority but that doesn't necessarily mean every moment has to be devoted to that. How can you judge whether the sacrifices in time and connection are acceptable or make the position wrong for you in this season? I do not know if I have all of the answers to that question.

For me, there has had to be faith involved. I have had to trust that if God is calling me, He will help me to ensure my family is okay. I still have the responsibility to manage my time and use wisdom in my day to day decision making. I get it wrong sometimes. There are seasons when my role takes me away from my family far more than I would like. I have moments of questioning those decisions and dealing with mum guilt. The firm belief that I am called to the roles I have provides the strength I need to move forward. I ask for forgiveness. I make changes where needed. At the end of the day, I release my family to God.

I have discovered that the impact on my family is inevitable. I have to make intentional choices to counteract the negative impact and press in to the positive. I have to set aside time to invest in my marriage. I try to do MOPS work at times when my daughter doesn't need me so that I can spend time connecting with her. A block schedule has helped with this. I have time slots in my calendar, blocked out for MOPS emails, meetings, phone calls and other work ,during school hours and after school activities. I have free space blocked after school pick up for us to do homework together, play Lego or go for a walk. I limit the number of evening meetings I have in a week and say no to extra social events at times to ensure I have several evenings free to spend with my husband —whether that is playing board games or watching a show together. There will still be times when I am away from my family. I have to make peace with that and be in communication with my husband and daughter to make it work. I have to hold on to the benefits that come from this too. More on that in the next chapter.

We each have finite time and resources at our disposal. Only you and your family can make the decision about whether those resources are available for leadership in this current season. It will require letting go of other roles, expectations and ways of doing things. The difficulty is trying to assess the impact of this before you have started living it. There will always be a level of faith and bravery involved as you have to make the leap and then figure it out day to day—no matter how much you have deliberated it before saying yes. Your family is on the journey of stretching and growing with you. You all feel the discomfort together and can move forward together.

He who calls you is faithful; He will surely do it.

1 Thessalonians 5:24 ESV

In the wrestle to decide whether I should step into the State Leader role, this Scripture hounded me. It would show up in random places, even on my daughter's music CD in the car! Maybe you need to be reminded that it is not about you but about God. He is the one who calls you into leadership and it is He who equips and brings those plans to reality. This reminder was what I needed to be able to say yes.

Leadership and motherhood: the challenges, joys and focus

The impact of my leadership on my daughter has been the greatest concern for me. I can talk issues through with my husband. He understands why I feel called and the decisions that I make through these discussions. It is more difficult with my daughter. Her understanding is limited and self-focused—even though she is a caring child— because of her age. There are times when MOPS to her is synonymous with Mummy leaving. I definitely spend more large blocks of time away from her than I ever have, with weekends away for training and conferences, and meetings during many evenings. If that was the only outcome of my leadership, it would not be worth the sacrifice.

Dealing with mum guilt is an ongoing battle for me as it is for many (maybe even most) mothers. There are times when my daughter is upset because I am leaving. There are times when I am on the phone or computer with MOPS business, even though I try to contain it to times when she is not around or involved with something else. It would be easy to wallow in that place of guilt if I didn't focus on the positive outcomes of being a mother who is in leadership.

If you have a daughter, you likely have similar hopes to me— you want her to grow up strong, with a compassionate heart and the skills to make an impact in her world. Children learn best through the modelling of the adults in their lives. I have the opportunity to show her how to work hard for a cause you believe in, how to be a leader and how to love the people in your life. I can show her how to make family a priority without having to sacrifice everything that you are and are called to. I can model my faith being worked out in real situations and show her what it looks like to seek guidance. I can model how to take care of myself physically, emotionally and mentally while serving in a role. I have to be practising all of these things in my own life to be able to demonstrate it to her. It is just as easy (or perhaps easier) to model unhealthy ways of leading, serving, overload and burn-out. Knowing those little eyes are watching stirs me to be a better leader.

I do not have a son but I imagine those same principles apply. Leadership skills are not limited to gender. There are core skills that need to be learned by all leaders. I also see a key opportunity to raise a man who is comfortable with a woman in leadership, who has seen how a woman can be strong and nurturing and invest both at home and outside the home.

I am blessed to be involved in an organisation that is geared to mothers being leaders. I am able to take my daughter along to meetings at times, and work around my family for the usual business of my weeks. The day to day choices come down to me being intentional with my time and being organised. I am far from where I want to be with this but I am a work in progress. There will be times when I get it wrong but there will also be times that will have a life-long impact for good on my daughter.

Your Turn

Take some time to reflect on what impact your current role or a potential role would have on your family and relationships. Think about both the positive and negative.

Assessing what you need to be a great leader

As I walk through this season of leadership, I have a strong desire to do this job well. I recognise that my current leadership skills have limitations and need to grow extensively. Perhaps you can relate to my sense of not even knowing what I do not know yet! There are some elements that are easy for me to identify, like conflict resolution. Other areas I have glimpses of but cannot define as yet. How do you know what to work on if you cannot even figure out what you need to learn? The longer I lead, the more I realise there is always more to learn.

I am far from having all the answers for this right now. I realise that I can only start with what I know and have open eyes and ears to learn as I go. Getting to know yourself and how you operate seems to be a logical place to start. That is what I have been doing— exploring my personality, my strengths and my weaknesses through doing assessments, reading and listening to podcasts. I have learned so much about myself. If you are like me and feeling overwhelmed with all that you have to learn, start with learning more about *you*.

Have you ever thought about how strange it is that the only person we are with every moment of everyday can still mystify us? We cannot escape from ourselves and yet our actions and thoughts can still confuse us. *Why did I say that? What made me respond like that? Why does that same issue keep coming back around?* When our actions and responses remain unexplored, we cannot hope to grow and change. I have been painfully and joyfully revealed to myself in personality assessments and in the words of leaders on podcasts and in books. I have discovered more of the ways in which I am wired and some of the common strengths and challenges that come with that. If I left it there, it would simply be an excuse to pull out for my behaviour.

Learning more about yourself is only a starting point. It gives you a starting point to grow in ways that are consistent with who you are, to begin to build on your strengths and work on the challenging areas. It has encouraged me to spend less time trying to be someone else and more time seeking to be more fully and healthily me. I used to wonder if the pursuit of knowing myself better was simply selfish and an exercise in navel gazing. I see how it can become that but I also see how unselfish it can be too. We can approach it from the perspective of wanting to be more fully who we are for the benefit of those around us and those we lead. I have often noted that the leaders I have observed doing the most damage seem to be the least self-aware. When we do not recognise our own actions and reactions and the drivers behind them, we cannot moderate the impact these have on others.

We can only go so far on our own in this endeavour. Others are often able to see things in us that we cannot see in ourselves. I am working on asking those close to me to speak into my leadership skills regularly. This takes courage and vulnerability. I want to foster a culture where those I have influence over can come to me about areas they feel need improvement. This requires wisdom and discernment on my part to see truth in what is spoken, and deal with unrealistic expectations and the tendency in me to people-please. I also seek out mentors, both for short seasons and more regular investment, to have another set of wise eyes looking at my life. Who are the people in your life who can invest in you and your leadership in this way? Perhaps it is time to make it a priority. Maybe there needs to be some professional coaching or counselling involved too.

We are blessed to live in a society that has ample access to resources. I am attending leadership conferences, reading books, listening to podcasts and spending time reflecting on that learning. This is in my nature. I process deeply and slowly. Spending time learning about the multitude of general skills in leadership will hopefully help to highlight specific areas I need to focus on. My challenge is to give time to this in the midst of the day to day work and the pull of distraction.

Leadership can only be done well with a mindset of life-long learning. We must grow and develop our skills as we go. I am in a position where I have head knowledge about many leadership skills. The application of that knowledge in the real world of your role is the key. I am up for the challenge. Are you?

Can introverts really be effective leaders? How do you take over from a different personality?

In the process of my own leadership journey, I discovered that I had a misconception about extroverts making better leaders. I felt that being an introvert had me at a disadvantage in leadership. I wasn't overly concerned about it until I was asked to take on a greater level of responsibility and influence. I was struggling to see how my personality would fit with the new position. Interacting with people drains me, even though I enjoy it and am drawn to that interaction (part of the dichotomy of my personality type, I have discovered). Holding conversation and talking on the phone can provoke anxiety in me. I struggle to maintain eye contact. How could I possibly run a ministry?

Being aware of the challenges I face as an introvert in leadership is important but not my main focus anymore. I want to identify areas to work on but also want to focus on the positives and advantages that my personality brings to the role. I started to research the personality classifications I had been learning about and their relationship to leadership. It gave me such a boost. I *do* have strengths that I *can* bring to leadership. I can help people feel heard and understood. I can connect with people. People with my personality tend to be good at inspiring people to embrace a vision and develop plans to carry that vision out. We tend to focus more on empowering those in our sphere of influence than seeking power and authority for ourselves. That sounds like a great potential for effective leadership.

I feel more capable of leadership after my research. I also recognise the potential pitfalls and want to equip myself to overcome these. If you are an introvert like me, I encourage you to learn more about your own personality and research it for yourself. You are able to be an effective leader. Each person brings to a team unique perspectives and strengths that combine for greater effectiveness.

A large part of the wrestle I had with accepting that my personality would not stop me from being an effective leader had been because of the difference in personality of the person that I was taking over from. I had the daunting privilege of taking over from someone who had been in the role for over ten years and was the first State Leader for MOPS in our state. Her leadership had been the only example that I had seen in this role.

I could not lead in the same way that she had, due to our very different natures and life circumstances. My initial reaction was to wonder how it could work differently. I had to step back and try to analyse what had been working well that I would like to emulate, and what changes could be made according to the way I am uniquely gifted and wired. I sensed a new season was on the horizon for MOPS in our state. This same process held true in the next role I took on, even though the person I took over from was far more like me in temperament. Every change requires a process and time of working through what it looks like for you, for this season, and for the current needs of where you are leading.

The next challenge I faced after resolving this wrestle in my own mind was how to help the people I lead to adjust to new ways of doing things. For some it was an easy change; for others, it was uncomfortable. I made mistakes. I intended to use my strengths of connecting with people and sharing my heart to ease this process, which I did at times and let fall by the wayside at others.

I have discovered that this part of the process is not a one time issue. Each step of the journey, each new approach or idea involves collaborating as a team and walking that out together. The only part of the process that I can fully control is me. I can focus on developing my own leadership skills and building relationships. You can guarantee that prayer is a considerable part of my strategy!

We now have this light
shining in our hearts, but we
ourselves are like fragile
clay jars containing this
great treasure. This makes it
clear that our great power is
from God, not from
ourselves.

2 Corinthians 4:7 NLT

This verse is like a sigh of relief for me. It's ok for me to be flawed, feel fragile at times and have areas of weakness. It is those imperfections that allow the glory of God to shine the brightest. It takes the pressure off me. I want the leadership work that I do to be empowered by God and point clearly to Him. I want people to wonder how I do it so that I can point them to God.

I pray that it encourages you the same way that it encourages me.

Conflict resolution: the area I was (and am) most nervous about

It will come as no surprise to those who know my personality that conflict resolution is the area that made me the most nervous in my new role. I usually avoid confrontation if at all possible, "the hedgehog approach" as the *Alpha* marriage course phrased it. I have long known this about myself. Being involved in conflict resolution is part of the job description for each role I have held. The difference now is that there are fewer and fewer people that I can pass it on to when it feels beyond my capacity!

Recognising this area of weakness within me over the past several years, in the context of work, church ministry and MOPS, I was faced with two choices: bury my head, keep using the same ineffective defences and at worst, allowing this to stop me saying yes to new leadership and work opportunities OR taking steps to grow in this area. I choose growth. I do not think I will ever get to the stage where I feel completely comfortable in confrontational situations. I can grow in confidence in my ability to speak into them, though.

When opportunities come up at conferences or in reading material to learn strategies around conflict resolution, especially within a Christian framework, I have been taking advantage of them. I have learned so much from this. I am also realising that my personality can be an asset in this area and not an obstacle as I have always viewed it. So much of what stands out to me in conflict resolution is the ability to connect with people, seek to understand different points of view and have the ability to step back and develop solutions. I have those skills.

Part of what makes confrontation difficult for me is that I can feel what other people are feeling in a way. I take on their emotions. The heightened emotion can leave me reeling and it takes an effort to process and engage my thoughts again. I have needed to develop strategies to give myself the space I need to process in order to be effective in working through the issues—with my brain fully active as well as being aware of my intuitive side.

As a Christian, the single greatest tool that I can employ is prayer. I have seen amazing heart changes and situation changes happen before I've even had the chance to meet with parties involved simply through prayer. There was one situation where I knew a leader needed to step down from her role. I just wasn't sure if she knew it too. I arranged to meet over coffee and prayed furiously in the days leading up to it. I felt the nausea rise up in anticipation of the potentially difficult conversation ahead but I went anyway. After a short time of catching up, she resigned from her role. There was no conflict or need for me to ask her to leave. There was only unity and peace. Prayer also changes me. I can be more at peace and recognise that I don't have to rely on my own wisdom and strength.

Maybe you are like me and struggle with confrontation. Maybe your issue with conflict resolution is completely different to mine. I encourage you to seek out guidance and teaching. This is a skill (or really a whole range of skills combined) that can be learned and utilised within the strengths and flavour that your personality brings.

Your Turn

Make a list of what you currently know about yourself and what you still want to work out. Reflect on how your personality and wiring contribute to your leadership.

What areas of your role or potential leadership roles worry you the most? Find one source of information you could engage with in order to address this area.

The pain and necessity of letting go

During a previous year's Write 31 Days challenge, I was writing on 'Increasing Capacity' on my blog and wrote a post on the importance of knowing when to let go of a role or other area of life. I was at the very start of this leadership journey in MOPS and had no concept of how the following years were going to progress. I have been in seasons of ever-increasing letting go ever since.

At the beginning of the year I took on the Region Leader role for MOPS, I stepped down from working in the children's ministry at my church and said no to all Sunday morning serving. This was different from how I had lived as part of a church community for most of my life. If I had based these decisions purely on a time commitment, I would not have felt the need to step down. It came down to headspace. All the different areas of my life take up real estate in my mind, even when I am not functioning in that area at the time. I may not be thinking of all of them in depth at all times but my focus is split often. They are always there in the background, requiring multiple focus shifts throughout my week. I realised quickly that this decreased my ability to be effective in all the areas. Some things had to go as new areas required greater space and focus.

That same factor of headspace came into play again as I stepped into each subsequent role. Even if all the time factors were covered (which they weren't realistically), my mind having to split and shift focus so frequently meant something or several things would suffer and be missed. I never wanted to do a job poorly for the sake of hanging on to it. I saw this starting to happen and the time had come to step down from some things to allow a greater capacity for stepping up in other areas.

There was pain to face in this process. The relief to my headspace came at a cost to my heart. The areas and roles that needed to be let go were not superfluous, disliked or of no value. It was a pruning process of cutting away what was good to make space for the best in the next season. This same truth has remained each time I have faced letting go.

When I stepped up into the State Leader role, the area I most needed to step down from was my original role at my local MOPS group. This was a huge part of my community and my weekly rhythms. It was where my MOPS leadership journey began. It was where I had formed deep friendships. Letting go of this role had the added connotations of friendships changing in how we connected and the times we have together as well as my usual term-time routine shifting and becoming more changeable.

It was further complicated by the difficulty we had in finding someone to step into the role. I desperately wanted to see this role filled with the right person who could develop it and make it her own, who could bring fresh passion to it. I had to trust that God would raise up that person even if it was not apparent at that moment. I had to continue to take steps to wrap up my time in that role regardless. There was a type of grief involved in this and I know that others felt that as well. The feeling of letting others down still rose up at times.

Aside from recognising the necessity of this process in order to lead well, I drew another consolation. By stepping out of a role at the right time, I allowed someone else to step up and continue on their own journey of leadership. I was not going to block the pathway for someone else. I may not have been able to name who that might be, but I was confident that they were out there and would be found in God's timing. His timing rarely coincides with what I would like it to be. There is faith and trust developed in the waiting. (God was faithful in providing that person, by the way.)

I hope that as you read, you have been able to recognise areas that you need to let go of. It may not be a role in this season. Maybe it is a letting go of certain expectations that you hold for yourself or others. Maybe it is a distraction that eats away your time. I know that the process can be painful but it is vital to leading well and stepping up to the next level of your leadership.

Your Turn

Take an honest look at your life right now. What do you need to let go of in order to free up headspace and be effective in what you do?

Leading myself by driving my faith deeper

The most important person for me to lead is myself. If I am not in a healthy place, all aspects of my leadership and life will suffer. I feel the weight of responsibility of leading a ministry at a national level. I am responsible for choosing new leaders for state and regional positions, directing the vision and focus of our organisation under the guidance of the Managing Director, and discerning and resolving issues. All of these things require the ability to hear from God. I was on a journey of drawing closer to God before being in this leadership position. Now I feel the urgency and necessity of that increasing. I cannot be effective in this position with lukewarm faith and a mediocre relationship with God.

Establishing a daily habit of spending time with God has been critical to developing that deeper relationship with Him. I am now in a season where I am feeling called to explore different ways to spend time with Him and hear from Him. I love Bible study and like to study in depth. I have discovered that I cannot restrict myself to this, however, as my relationship was growing stale and becoming more of an intellectual pursuit. What I was craving was connection with Him by spending time in His presence.

I have been exploring contemplative prayer techniques used for centuries in traditional churches. I have grown up in charismatic and modern churches, for want of a better phrase. I have loved this but sense that there is so much to be gained from combining some of the practices used by other denominations, to provide a richer and more well-rounded experience of God. These times of silence, of *Examen*, of *Lectio Divina*, of centring prayer, are allowing me to connect with God in new ways. I still journal my prayers and make requests of God but that has become less dominant in my prayer time. I am far from an expert or even consistent with these practices as yet. Having a small child who rises very early and a small house where quiet spaces are hard to find create challenges but these are not insurmountable.

After attending the Global Leadership Summit, I started to include a short leadership reflection during many of my morning times with God. This has helped me to keep my faith and leadership journey linked and reminds me to bring God into every aspect of my leadership. It encourages me to take brave steps and stretch past what I am comfortable with, as I am assured of God's presence with me. The foundational truths in Scripture help to keep my mindset fixed where it needs to be.

My relationship with God is dynamic, creative, growing and deepening. Like any relationship, it requires investment to stay healthy. That looks different in the different days and seasons of life. What works at one time may not fit or produce the same closeness at another. I need to be open to new ways of spending time with Him. This is the next step in my journey of faith to create a deeper relationship with God. Yours may look different. Wherever you are at in your faith journey, look for that next step to take. God is passionate about connecting with us but we are usually the ones too distracted or set on keeping Him small in our lives. No one else can make these choices or develop your faith for you.

Your Turn

What does your faith journey look like at this point in time? What next steps do you see in front of you to move forward and deeper with this?

Leading myself by prioritising rest

No one else can make the choice to rest for you. There are a myriad of demands and distractions that want to pull you from that choice. How much priority do you give to rest and what impact does that have on your leadership capacity? What does rest look like in your season of life?

It seems counterintuitive to take time out to pursue rest when your to-do list is ever increasing. Many people, including myself, have found that productivity and effectiveness is boosted by rest. Our world promotes more and more hustle; do more, connect more, be more involved, be all things to all people. We were not designed to function this way. I think we are especially susceptible to this expectation as women. We want to do and have it all. The downside of the wins of feminism, perhaps. It takes an intentional choice to lay down these expectations we place on ourselves and choose to take care of our souls.

Rest is part of that work of caring for your soul. When you recognise that it is just as much about your soul as your body, your view of what is restful can shift too. Rest for you may look like cooking a special meal, reading a book, writing, painting, watching a show that you love, talking to a friend, sitting on a beach, hiking through the woods. The possibilities are endless. What do you find restful that you may not have viewed as rest before?

I would love to say that I have mastered prioritising rest. I have come a long way but have a tendency to switch into rest that doesn't actually restore my soul. Watching one episode of a show may provide a welcome brain break but this can quickly turn to binge watching that drains and adds time pressure. Carving out time to write fills a deep need within but doing that at the expense of relationship time with my daughter leaves me drained by a conviction of my actions and by the meltdowns that ensue when she hasn't had her connection tank filled. This is the area of rest that I now need to work on.

I have started to implement rhythms of rest in my week. I choose to rise early most mornings to sit in the quiet, journal and connect with God. I swim laps twice a week, creating space for my mind to think, my soul to process and my body to release stress. I detour for a longer walk on my way back from school drop off, aiming for at least once a week. I love to read—escaping into fictional worlds and digging deep into learning from leadership books too. I listen to podcasts that ignite my passion, give me ideas and encourage me. I take breaks from my phone and the noise of social media at scheduled parts of my day and week. Crochet projects, a sticker mosaic book, and colouring books sit beside my favourite spot in the lounge for easy access in those moments of downtime. This rhythm of rest also includes times of watching YouTube, playing games on my phone and watching a show on Netflix but I find myself feeling less rested internally when I allow these to be my primary downtime activities.

Having the view of rest as a rhythm over my days and weeks has helped me to place priority on it. I see it as a natural part of the flow of my life and feel the benefits to the rest of my week when I go with that rhythm and do not resist it. It allows for both the small windows of time within my day and the larger, more intentional blocks of downtime to be included. The routine of when I wake, when I eat and when I go to bed provides a framework for getting the physical rest and recharging I need that are the foundation for the soul rest practices. Look at your own day and week. Where are the natural opportunities for implementing a rhythm of rest? What do you need to change in order to recharge your body and soul?

Your Turn

What types of activities are restful to you in this season? Make a plan for how you will include those times of rest into your weekly rhythm. (You might want to block out the time in your calendar too.)

Leading myself by taking care of my body

A few years ago, I was listening to a Christine Caine podcast series on leadership during which she was talking about the importance of taking care of ourselves physically as leaders. I didn't act on this immediately but it stuck with me. I knew that I was not eating well or exercising and not in peak health. If you have ever considered making significant changes to your lifestyle, you will know that it can take a while to be in the right headspace to implement changes. It wasn't until I was asked to step up into a Region Leader position that I started to consider changes seriously.

Those who know me in real life have seen evidence of these changes over the following years. I feel strongly that in order to be truly effective as a leader, I need to give my body the best access to energy and health as is in my control. I am far from perfect in this area but I am not aiming for perfection. I am aiming for long term lifestyle change. A deviation here and there does not have to derail my goals completely. I am aiming for health and energy. Weight loss is an added bonus but not my focus. I think that is part of what is making the changes more sustainable. My priorities are in the right place.

Changes to my eating habits have made the most significant difference. I follow an eating plan called *Trim Healthy Mama* that is designed to be a long-term lifestyle change. A friend of mine had switched to this way of eating and suggested it. I was drawn to their philosophy of food freedom and focus on health and energy, as much as weight loss. The basic premise of the plan is having protein with every meal and snack, separating fats and carbs while in the weight loss phase and regular eating to keep up your metabolism. This way of eating cuts out sugar —which is hard but feels so good when I stick to it. The long-term approach rather than a diet has helped because it allows me leeway to be 'off plan' for a meal without feeling derailed like breaking a diet would. I aim to eat 'on plan' for 80% of my meals and snacks. This gives me space for the unexpected or special events. Whatever eating plan you gravitate towards, it is the lifestyle change that you are aiming for over quick weight loss with unsustainable ways of eating.

Tiredness and lethargy have long been enemies of mine. Being the mother of a young child, especially one who has been averse to sleep her entire life, is exhausting. There are many steps that I can take to put myself in the best possible space. I can ensure that I am getting to bed at a reasonable time. I can fuel my body with food that will give longer term energy rather than quick fixes. I can exercise to keep myself strong and increase energy levels.

Exercise took longer to be consistent with than eating for me. The change actually came through a significant injury. A split second slip down the ladder in our camper trailer resulted in a major tear through a rotator cuff muscle in my right shoulder. I later found out that it was likely dislocated when I fell but popped back into place by itself. That would explain the blinding pain I was in! I started with physiotherapy as soon as we got back home but ended up needing surgery to repair the damage. Despite being dedicated to my rehabilitation program, I developed a complication called 'frozen shoulder'. It is now eighteen months since surgery and I am finally at the recovery stage I should have been at six months post surgery.

The motivation to recover my function and be as pain free as possible spurred me on. This regular rhythm of rehabilitation exercises in my days and the addition of regular swimming to strengthen my shoulder have been key to consistency with exercise. I have found another source of motivation for walking too. I wish I could say that it was the prayer times I have or simply the enjoyment of nature. Those are true once I get out but often do not spur me on initially. I play a game requires you to walk and go to different locations to play. I get rewarded for how much I walk each week. It has the added benefit of time with my daughter for some of the walks, as she enjoys playing the game too. Whatever your exercise rhythm, find something that is fun to you and find what will motivate you—although I wouldn't recommend the serious injury catalyst if you can avoid it!

Maybe this is an area that you haven't previously considered as being part of your leadership. How are you tracking with taking care of yourself physically? I have experienced the benefit of making changes. I can see the impact on my ability to sustain my energy levels in order to lead well. Maybe the key for you is to adopt the long-term view as I have been seeking to do. I encourage you to consider one change you could put in place to take care of yourself physically over this next season.

Your Turn

Spend time reflecting honestly on how you are taking care of yourself physically. Choose 1-2 changes that you want to make and take action.

What challenges do you face in leading yourself?

The idea of leading ourselves being the most valuable and most difficult element of our leadership has been resonating with me. The reality is that the only person I can truly seek to control and change is myself. I have spent time reflecting on some of those ways in which I have been seeking to lead myself. Now, I want to talk about those areas that continue to challenge and frustrate me. Whenever I contemplate these issues, the verses that Paul wrote in Romans come to mind.

14-16 I can anticipate the response that is coming: "I know that all God's commands are spiritual, but I'm not. Isn't this also your experience?" Yes. I'm full of myself—after all, I've spent a long time in sin's prison. What I don't understand about myself is that I decide one way, but then I act another, doing things I absolutely despise. So if I can't be trusted to figure out what is best for myself and then do it, it becomes obvious that God's command is necessary.

17-20 But I need something more! For if I know the law but still can't keep it, and if the power of sin within me keeps sabotaging my best intentions, I obviously need help! I realize that I don't have what it takes. I can will it, but I can't do it. I decide to do good, but I don't really do it; I decide not to do bad, but then I do it anyway. My decisions, such as they are, don't result in actions. Something has gone wrong deep within me and gets the better of me every time.

—*Romans 7:15-20 The Message (MSG)*

The biggest ongoing struggle for me is giving in to the pull of distraction and technology that eats up my time and prevents me from being truly present in many moments of my day. I first wrote about these struggles on my blog years ago and still I battle on. I know that I am not alone in this struggle and that it is an ever increasing problem in our world. Technology can have so many benefits and brilliant uses in our leadership but can cut down our effectiveness if not managed. I wish I could say that I have this mastered.

I have been reminded again of the impact of leaving this unchecked when my daughter starts playing with her 'phone' while we're at the table so that she can "just check this message quickly," and pretends to finish her meal quickly so she can get back to her 'phone'. A punch in the gut! I see my own behaviour held up in a mirror. This has been the wake up call to make changes.

Any changes that I make in this area usually prove short lasting. I continue to try new strategies to break these patterns of behaviour. Habits and addictive behaviours are never conquered in one hit. It takes daily intention, alternative options and supports to make it last. In a talk I give at MOPS groups titled 'Confessions of a Phone Addicted Mum', I identify three roots that need to be tackled in different ways —overwhelm, the need for connection and habit. When overwhelm is dominant, I need to go back to what is truly restful, taking care of myself and adjusting my schedule to ensure I am creating space in my weeks. When the need for connection is driving my phone use, I need to seek out opportunities for real connection not the illusion of connection found in scrolling social media. Habit requires using a program like *Offtime* to lock down my phone and keep me from mindlessly checking my phone constantly. I now have a toolbelt of strategies to draw from.

Those Romans verses remind me that change in my own strength is not possible. This has to be a spiritual battle for me too. I have to be willing to continue to submit to God and not ignore His promptings during my day to change behaviour. It is in His strength that I can make progress. The practice of regular connection with God provides the foundation I need.

What is it in your own life that feels like a deep dark secret or feels like a battle that continues to rage despite all your best efforts? What are those challenges that you face in trying to lead yourself? Can you relate to my frustration and the truth of self-leadership being the most difficult to achieve? We may all have different issues that we are facing but we are united in our humanity. It is such a relief to have access to God's grace. My tendency is to beat myself up over my struggles. I sense God looking down at me, not with anger but with love, encouraging me as a father. His love is patient and slow to anger. Do you take your issues to God and ask for His help or does shame hold you back? He is waiting to help.

I am realising that my part of self-leadership is an honest evaluation of myself. Sometimes this requires an honest evaluation from someone else too—a mentor or coach who will not let you hide behind excuses and defensiveness. Then it is taking steps of obedience in any problems that arise, working hard but more importantly, drawing near to God. He performs the transformation within.

Your Turn

Spend some time reflecting on those areas in your own life that are the most challenging to master.

My people are essential to my leadership

The more responsibility I take on in leadership, the more I value the close friendships and family I have. Their encouragement, prayers and practical help keep me going. They challenge me when I need to be challenged. They bring correction. They celebrate with me and cheer me on. It takes effort and intentional choice to invest in these relationships when it would be easier to bury myself in everything on my to-do list. I need to remember how much I need them.

I love that I have people I can message when I'm having a bad day and ask them to pray. They can do the same. They are my people, my tribe, my community. They keep me grounded and in touch. They enable me to get tasks done while my daughter is loved on and entertained. They believe in me when I struggle to believe in myself.

My parents will take my daughter for a sleep over while I'm away on a trip to distract her and love on her. I have a friend who is always baking healthy and delicious treats. She will randomly drop some off for me, having made a gluten and dairy free treat that my daughter and I can enjoy. I have another friend who is amazing with websites, design and planning. She has given up time in her own business schedule to help me work through problems on my website or give me feedback on a product I am creating. Yet another friend will call and ask to take my daughter for an afternoon to give me space to catch up on tasks that are piling up in a busy season.

My husband has been my continual support on this journey. He has taken time off work to allow me to go away numerous times a year to run leadership retreats and events. He does all of the grocery shopping so it is one less thing for me to fit in. He has never stood in the way when I have felt called to step up. His concerns are often about me and how I am coping. He brings me unexpected treats and shows in so many little ways that he cares and supports me. I am not always the easiest to live with and yet he loves me anyway.

When I reflect on all that my people do for me, it is impossible to imagine being in leadership without them. This is what drives me to keep building these relationships. I am far from perfect in this. I fail as a friend frequently. I get lost in my own introverted world. They forgive me and love me anyway. I cannot thank them enough.

Community doesn't just happen. It is impossible to build these relationships without giving them time and contact. It requires intentional choice to invest time out of our busy schedules. I used to struggle because there were so many people I was wanting to deepen friendships with but could not possibly spend time with them all. The overwhelm meant I withdrew from everyone. I am having to accept the reality that I can only invest fully in a few. Some friends are for a season and I have to be okay with recognising when a season has reached its end. I also value those friendships that can be picked up infrequently when the opportunity arises, that have a foundation of depth and history that allows us to reconnect quickly even if it is only once or twice a year.

How often do you invest in friendships and in your family? Have you let relationships slide as you step up in leadership? Who in your life is cheering you on, encouraging you, pushing you to improve? Have you thanked them recently? May we be the kind of leaders who see the value in our tribe and invest in that. May we be the kind of friends who carry out this vital role for others.

Your Turn

Take some time to answer those questions for yourself.

Are you tired? Worn out? Burned out
on religion? Come to me. Get away
with me and you'll recover your life.
I'll show you how to take a real rest.
Walk with me and work with me-
watch how I do it. Learn the unforced
rhythms of grace. I won't lay anything
heavy or ill-fitting on you. Keep
company with me and you'll learn to
live freely and lighly.

Matthew 11:28-30 MSG

I come back to these verses, the Message version in particular, frequently. I still do not fully understand how to live this out but I am learning. I have been in that place of feeling burned out from the doing. I recognise the tendency within me to return to that place. Real rest, unforced rhythms of grace, living freely and lightly are all available to me through walking with Jesus, just being with Him. This is what I want my life and my leadership journey to look like. This is what I want for you, too.

Empowering those you have influence over

One of the aspects of my role in MOPS that I have loved exploring and developing is calling other women into leadership. When I think of the highlights from the past year, some of the standout moments have been when women, in whom I see leadership potential, step up despite their fears. I love that the journey I have been on, confronting feelings of inadequacy and wrestling with taking on the label of a leader, is producing fruit in the lives of others. I am able to encourage and share from an authentic heart as I know what that is like. What a privilege to be able to speak and pray into someone else's journey.

A huge part of my heart and vision for this next season of my own leadership journey is empowering others. For our ministries to flourish and grow to another level, we need more leaders operating in their full capacity. We need a diversity of leaders all bringing their unique personalities and gifts. I cannot do it all and nor should I. The Biblical model is a body of diverse parts working together. We miss out on so much when people choose to let fear or busyness keep them from leadership. In saying this, I understand and completely agree with the women I speak to who decide that a leadership position is not a 'best yes' for them at that time. I wonder, though, if some of them say no because they doubt their capacity or fail to recognise their own calling.

I found in my own life and see in others that the season of being a mother of young children is a time when it is easy to lose yourself. It is common in this season to feel unable to lead, or be part of anything. So much of our capacity is taken up by the everyday relentlessness of our children's needs. I often felt stuck and frustrated. MOPS gave me the opportunity to step up, even in my more limited capacity. I found that my capacity grew as I took those steps. I long to encourage other women who may be feeling the same. I see so much potential in the women I meet in MOPS and other spaces. The battle is often getting them to see it for themselves. I have experienced the significance of others calling out the leadership potential they saw in me, by inviting me to new positions and articulating the reasons why. I want to do the same for others.

I do not have a formula for how to do this. I wish it was a simple process. Relationship is often the key. Repeated opportunities to speak encouragement, share my own journey, extend invitations and walk alongside someone build up to the moment when they can say yes. It will look different with each person. This has to be guided by God. The times when I have seen the process succeed is when it was first seeded in my heart during times of prayer and hanging out in God's presence. Prayer covers each step. Trust is involved. As well as trusting God to show His strength in their weakness, these women must trust that you will walk with them and support them in their leadership journey. I want to be a leader that others can trust to do this.

I have a sense of anticipation in my heart to see how God brings together teams, builds existing leaders and propels them forward over the coming years. Leadership is this cyclical journey. Others invest in us. We step up and invest in others. Those people then step up and invest in the people they have influence over. The movement of leadership swells and washes over a greater number of people. It only works as each of us say yes to our part and take responsibility to lead well.

Discovering vision for where I lead

I never considered myself a visionary. Maybe you do not think that about yourself either. Saying yes to a role that asks you to direct others in vision and focus is incredibly daunting—at least it was for me. I think I believed that you either were a visionary who could do this or you weren't. I still believe that it is a more natural gifting for some. I have come to realise through experience that, like all leadership skills, it can be learned and developed. I think back to when I was first writing about this topic in the blog series that started this book and it makes me smile. I left it to the last week of the month, hoping I would discover something that I could write while I was preparing for a team retreat that had 'vision setting' as one of its goals. Thankfully, I was right.

Preparing for the team retreat, I spent time with God seeking His heart for MOPS in Western Australia. In my life in Christian ministry, seeking

God is where vision begins. God came through. Fragments of thought from previous weeks and months consolidated. He dropped a phrase into my heart that encompassed what was needed in the coming season. I wouldn't have received this answer if I hadn't created the space to listen. If you are struggling to set a vision, maybe you need to do more listening and sitting in God's presence.

Through this process, I recognised that my fear about the responsibility of setting vision was unfounded. I have sought and set the vision for areas I've been responsible for and for my own life without attaching that label to it. I also realised that my part of the equation is making space for God to speak, and using the observation and discernment skills he has already placed within me. *He* is the one who sets the vision. I need only hear it and communicate it.

As I reflected on times in the past where I have used this process without realising it, I had an epiphany. I realised that I frequently sense seasons that are ahead, for myself or for areas I lead in. Vision is wrapped up in the concept of seasons for me. The phrase that I settled on for the season ahead of this retreat? 'Shore up the foundations'. There was obviously a lot of detail to draw out around this idea but this provided the overview of what I felt we needed to focus on for the next season. I also had a personal sense of being called into a season of transition. That may seem obvious when moving into a new role but it went deeper than that. It was a sense of being a transitional person providing the bridge between the one who had gone before me and the one who would come after me. Of course, I did not realise at the time that it was also talking about transitioning me to a place where I could step up yet again!

Vision will likely look different to you. We are all wired in unique ways and connect with and hear from God in different ways as well. God speaks to me with a sense of seasons and words to go with that. Sometimes it involves a picture as well. Maybe for you, the images are stronger or you have broad strokes of vision that need others to come alongside and fill in details. Maybe you see leaps and bounds ahead with huge grand plans that need your team to develop stepping stones towards. Maybe you do not know what that looks like yet. My encouragement to you is to start paying attention in your own life. Tune in to how you make plans for yourself and how you look ahead. Then simply carve out time to listen and dream, and practise drawing out vision.

Having a vision is one thing. Developing strategies to see this vision come to life is key. While I have some ideas about this, I recognise that I need my team around me to flesh it out. It is a vision for *our* ministry and it will be *our* strategies and combined ideas that will work it out. This requires me to communicate that vision to them.

Communicating the vision to others

I am still on a learning curve when it comes to communicating vision. I share with you some of what I have learned so far. That first team retreat gave me the opportunity to engage in this process for the first time. My hope was that the passion I felt for this vision would transmit through my words. I had to trust that God would be preparing hearts and igniting the vision within the team, as He had in me. This process was made easier knowing that the team was already passionate about what we do.

I needed clarity in my own mind to be able to communicate the vision effectively. I researched definitions, sought the right words and wrote down notes on what I wanted to say. I was feeling confident in being able to bring an understanding of what God had laid on my heart. I had the 'umbrella' of the vision for our ministry for the next season.

I knew that there was much that still needed to be fleshed out as we began to implement strategies and plan for events for the next year. My desire was for the team to be a large part of that process, allowing it to be more fully their vision. I needed everyone on the team to contribute their unique perspectives, abilities and ideas to succeed in driving our ministry forward. I was looking forward to discussing the plans and vision with my team.

It is one thing to be confident in what you've heard when you are by yourself. It is another to hold on to that when facing other people. God had it under control. The test of the vision, in my opinion, is how it resonates with other key stakeholders. The truth of what God had spoken to me was evident as it resonated with the team and confirmed ideas that they had been thinking over. As we discussed the implications of this vision for the next year and what that could look like, I saw the fire catching in their hearts. I saw the unique giftings and viewpoints emerging to form a solid plan for achieving this vision. It struck me again how my part is to be listening and obedient to speak what God has said to me. God does the rest in developing the vision in others. This has proven true in subsequent discussions of vision and changes with my team over the years. While change is never comfortable and some feel called to step out of their role, the ultimate response from the core leaders has been in full support as the vision aligns with their own.

The challenge moving forward will always be holding this vision myself and keeping it at the forefront of my team's focus over the whole year or season. Several leadership teachers use the term 'vision leaks'. It is human nature to get caught up in our everyday lives and lose that first passion and momentum. It is my responsibility to keep coming back to what God has placed on my heart and reminding my team of this. Maybe it would help to 'write it on my walls' where I would see it in my daily life.

Your Turn

Reflect on the ways that you engage with vision in your own life. What does that look like for you?

How can you communicate vision to the key people involved?

What strategies will you use to keep the vision fresh in mind for you and for your leaders?

Giving up on long-term planning

It may seem odd to follow chapters where I have reflected on setting a vision and communicating that vision with a chapter about giving up on long-term planning. Allow me to explain. For the past few years, every long-term plan I have made and every idea for the future I have had has been blown out of the water. My life today is far different from what I thought it would be. This may sound negative, but it is quite the opposite. I have experienced time and again that the plans that God brings about in my life may be challenging, but are far more beneficial than anything I could have come up with.

I am learning more and more that I try to control my anxiety by making plans. If my husband is running late and I start feeling flickers of anxiety about his safety, my mind defaults to planning for how I would cope without him, who I would call first if a policeman showed up on my doorstep, how I would go about paying for a funeral. All of these thoughts are attempts to feel in control. I am realising that it comes down to a lack of trust.

It is this lack of trust that I am working on. Giving up on long-term planning is not a matter of throwing my hands up in defeat but a conscious opening of my hands to let go. As I draw closer in my relationship with God, I trust Him more. I am able to trust that the path He has me on is for my good and for His purposes. I am learning to be content with knowing just the next step in front of me. I continue to seek out the seasons He has on the way for me but I am working on releasing the need to know details and plans for months and years ahead.

How does this relate to my leadership journey? Well, none of the leadership steps I have taken has been planned by me. Each has taken me by surprise in many ways. I have no idea how long I will be in this role and what will come after it. Amazingly for me, I am at peace with that. My default (that still tries to rear up at times) is to spend time, headspace and emotional energy working out many different scenarios and possibilities. That achieves nothing except to serve as a distraction from the present. I want to be fully present in my life today, investing that time and energy into my family first and foremost and then into my team, my responsibilities and my leadership skills.

Giving up on long-term planning is necessary for my leadership to allow me to walk in trust and be flexible. Maybe you can relate to that. Maybe for you, long-term planning is not a distraction but a skill that you need to work on. Perhaps your lack of organisation and forward thinking are the areas that are holding you back in your leadership journey. We are each unique in what we need to let go of and what we need to pursue.

So how do you take responsibility by planning and getting organised while still creating the space for God to move and change direction? There are numerous approaches to goal setting and project management and I encourage you to explore the options and find what works for you best. I am currently getting organised by plotting out the big events and projects over the year, including the space I need to prepare in the lead up. I am using block scheduling in both my paper planner and digital calendar to know what I am focusing on in that time slot of the day. I am developing systems in online project management tools that help me track all of the details of the planning. I am working on my delegation skills, seeking to ensure I am setting those people up for success. I endeavour to stick to the set weekly rhythms and work towards those project goals consistently over time.

One key I have found is to hold these plans loosely in many ways and have strategies in place to hand over to another leader if needed. By staying tuned in to where God is leading and the feedback of those I lead, I can make course corrections as we go. Sometimes a project I have set needs to be laid down for a time or for good. I have to be willing to let go. It takes humility and flexibility. In my experience, it's often more about my perspective and internal posture than about the practical plans. Let us learn to live well in the place of tension between being organised and remaining fluid, so that we can flow in the direction needed for ourselves and our organisations to flourish.

Those who live in the shelter of the Most
High
will find rest in the shadow of the
Almighty. This I declare about the Lord:
He alone is my refuge, my place of safety;
he is my God, and I trust him. For he will
rescue you from every trap and protect
you from deadly disease. He will cover
you with his feathers. He will shelter you
with his wings. His faithful promises are
your armor and protection.

Psalm 91: 1-4 NLT

These verses have long been among my favourites. They combine the messages of abiding, rest and feathers that God has been talking to me about over the past few years. I am learning more and more that my leadership ability is going to be directly proportional to how much I am living in Christ. These verses feel like a wrap-around blanket of peace.

The next steps on your leadership journey

The fact that you have read this book tells me that you are a leader on a journey, just like I am. Maybe you are uncomfortable with that title—but you are a leader, whether you have an official position or not. You are a leader in your family, in your community, your workplace or in your ministry. The question now is, what will you do with that leadership journey? It comes down to a choice to embrace it with all its ups and downs, its sacrifices and challenges, its elation and hard work—or to fight against it and limit the impact you could have.

What element discussed in this book stood out to you? What captured your attention? Often that is a good indicator of where your heart is at and what you are needing to focus on. I encourage you to take the time to think about these concepts. Take time to listen to God regularly and draw closer to Him. Read and listen to books and podcasts that speak into leadership skills and areas that you want to develop in. Search for people around you who can mentor you, encourage you or keep you accountable. Only you can choose to listen and determine the next step in your leadership journey.

If you are interested in staying in touch with my journey and reading more about what I learn and ponder on, you can connect with me through-
Facebook: @jokoepke
Instagram: @jokoepke
Website: www.jokoepke.com

My heart is to continue to encourage and inspire other leaders on their journey through what I learn on mine.

ACKNOWLEDGEMENTS

I have procrastinated writing this section. How do you find adequate words to convey your appreciation to all the people who have brought you to this point where these words have formed a book and that book is about to be released into the world? I am anxious not to miss someone too!

I cannot start anywhere but with my family. From my parents, Terry and Lynne, who have raised me with the support and belief that I could be brave and be me to my husband, Andreas, who is my partner and safe place to my daughter, Isabel, who is my most enthusiastic cheerleader. Words will never be enough.

I couldn't possibly name all the friends who have cheered me on, encouraged me, read my words and supported me. Thank you to each and every one of you, especially my Friday catch up crew.

Thanks to Tiffany Edmonds, a fellow Hope*writer, who helped with early feedback and edits and suggested adding in the sections for reflection.

Thanks to Lexia Smallwood for her edits and input as well as for her leadership. Thanks also to all of MOPS Australia and the leaders past and present who have helped to develop me to this point and will continue to do so in the future.

Thanks to my editor, Emma-Lee Hazeldean. I needed your eyes and help to make the message clear.

Thanks to Melissa Shanhun for your help in planning out my time, your encouragement and technical support with websites, Leadpages and Photoshop.

Thanks to Amanda Viviers for your mentoring around planning out this project and advice on self-publishing.

I am blessed to be part of some online and in-person communities that have grown me as a writer and a creative—Hope*writers, Write 31 Days, Five Minute Friday and the Inspire Collective.

And now to you, my reader. I am constantly humbled to think that you would use your time and money to read my words. You have been at the forefront of my mind in all of my writing. These words are for your encouragement and growth. I can only offer them to you. You are the one who needs to take the lessons and run with them. I'm cheering for you.

www.ingramcontent.com/pod-product-compliance
Lightning Source LLC
Chambersburg PA
CBHW072106040426
42334CB00042B/2494

"This journey has ignited a passion for leadership within me and a passion to bring other women like me along for the ride."

Struggling to accept the label of 'leader' in your life? Feeling out of your depth? Wonder when you will be free from feeling inadequate or like an imposter?

Jo knows what that feels like. She shares lessons she has learned in the rocket blast of leadership over the past few years.

Find lessons and reflections on:
• what leadership is
• what drives you, including the shadow side
• barriers, challenges and impacts of leadership
• leading yourself
• supports in leadership
• developing and holding vision

Use the 'Your turn' pages to reflect on how these lessons apply in your own life.

This book will leave you equipped and encouraged to step up in your own leadership journey, and to learn how to lead yourself and others well.

"So practical and engaging that it is really easy to read. There is no fluff or padding—just simple, concise information, challenges and encouragement. And more than just easy to read—I found many of the observations and discoveries resonated with me."
Lexia Smallwood, Managing Director MOPS Australia

Jo Koepke is a writer and speaker, living in Perth, Western Australia with her family. She is Field Manager for MOPS Australia. Her regular writing can be found on jokoepke.com.

ISBN 978-0-646-80351-7
90000

9 780646 803517